at the feet of
the master
and towards
discipleship

at the feet of the master and towards discipleship

Jiddu Krishnamurti

(Alcyone)

Quest Books
Theosophical Publishing House
Wheaton, Illinois ♦ Chennai (Madras), India

The Theosophical Society wishes to acknowledge
the generous support of the Kern Foundation in
the publication of this book.

New Quest edition, revised and expanded

The Theosophical Publishing House
P. O. Box 270
Wheaton, IL 60189-0270

Library of Congress Cataloging-in-Publication Data

Krishnamurti, J. (Jiddu).
At the feet of the master and towards discipleship / Jiddu
Krishnamurti (Alcyone) — New quest ed., rev. and enl.
            p.   cm.
Includes bibliographical references.
ISBN 0-8356-0803-4
1. Theosophy.   I. Title

BP565.K7 A48 2001
299'.934 — dc21

                                        2001019790

    6 5 4 3 2 1 * 01 02 03 04 05 06

Printed in the United States of America

To

Those Who Knock

From the unreal lead me to the Real.

From darkness lead me to Light.

From death lead me to Immortality.

Contents

List of Illustrations

at the feet of the master

The Origin of This Book

It was a hot summer evening in 1909. The famous clairvoyant Charles Webster Leadbeater, who had returned to Adyar earlier that year, had gone to the beach to swim in the warm waters of the Bay of Bengal. On returning, he remarked to his assistant, Ernest Wood, that on the beach he had seen a boy with the most remarkable aura he had ever observed, one with no taint of selfishness in it. When Wood learned the identity of the lad with the wonderful aura, he was amazed because, having tried to tutor that very boy in his studies, Wood had concluded he must be retarded.

When Wood told Leadbeater his impressions of the boy, the old man insisted that the youngster would grow into a spiritual teacher and a world-renowned speaker. "How great?" asked Wood, "As great as Mrs. Besant?" "Much greater," was Leadbeater's reply. Wood shook his head in disbelief. The boy was unprepossessing in the extreme. He was sickly, scrawny, grubby, and infested with lice. He had crooked teeth and a vacant expression in his eyes. The front of his head was shaved in the local native manner, and the hair at the back worn in a pigtail. A less likely spiritual teacher and world orator would be hard to imagine.

Leadbeater, however, was not deterred from his vision of the boy's potential. Indeed, he informed Wood that this ragamuffin of a young teenager, who had just turned fourteen, was destined to become, "unless something went wrong," the means by which a great teaching would be given to the world and that he, Leadbeater, was to prepare him for that destiny. He began that preparation by clairvoyantly investigating the past lives of the boy, who for that purpose was given the "star name" *Alcyone,* the brightest star of the Pleiades, to designate the reincarnating individuality behind the present personality named *Krishnamurti.*

Leadbeater did more than look at Alcyone's past lives. He set about to transform Krishnamurti's present life suitably for the great future he saw ahead. He prescribed the boy's diet, gave him a regimen of exercise, introduced him to Western customs of bathing and grooming, and assigned him to Ernest Wood for instructions in English and other school subjects. He ran Krishnamurti and his brother Nitya through as rigorous a system of education as any English public school could boast of, teaching them to sit, eat, sleep, and dress like proper Victorian young gentlemen.

Krishnamurti's spiritual development was not slighted either. Only a few months after he had assumed direction over the boys' progress, Leadbeater reported that he had taken the two brothers in their astral bodies, while their physical forms slept, to present them to the great soul who was his own Master, who put them both on probation as his pupils. Every night for the next five months, Leadbeater took Krishnamurti astrally to the Master, who gave the boy a short instruction, ending with a few memorable lines of summary. Every morning when he woke, the boy wrote down what he could remember of that instruction. Several persons observed him so writing.

The records of remembered instructions were gathered together, spelling and punctuation errors corrected but the text otherwise unchanged, and the result was published late the following year as a slim little volume called *At the Feet of the Master*. It has not been out of print since then and has appeared in many forms. What follows is the instruction of one of the Wise ones of our kind to a teenager who had to be prepared for a great future before him.

John Algeo, 2001

Foreword

The privilege is given to me, as an elder, to pen a word of introduction to this little book, the first written by a younger brother, young in body verily, but not in soul. The teachings contained in it were given to him by his Master in preparing him for initiation, and were written down by him from memory —slowly and laboriously, for his English last year was far less fluent than it is now. The greater part is a reproduction of the Master's own words; that which is not such a verbal reproduction is the Master's thought clothed in his pupil's words. Two omitted sentences were supplied by the Master. In two other cases an omitted word has been added. Beyond this, it is entirely Alcyone's own, his first gift to the world.

May it help others as the spoken teachings helped him—such is the hope with which he gives it. But the teaching can only be fruitful if it is lived, as he has lived it, since it fell from the Master's lips. If the example be followed as well as the precept, then for the reader, as for the writer, shall the great Portal swing open, and his feet be set on the Path.

Annie Besant, 1910

Foreword

[In this 2001 edition, capitalization has been modernized and the language has been slightly adjusted to reflect current preferences for word choice in some cases.]

Preface

These are not my words; they are the words of the Master who taught me. Without him I could have done nothing, but through his help I have set my feet upon the Path. You also desire to enter the same Path, so the words which he spoke to me will help you also, if you will obey them. It is not enough to say that they are true and beautiful; a person who wishes to succeed must do exactly what is said. To look at food and say that it is good will not satisfy those who are starving;

they must put forth their hands and eat. So to hear the Master's words is not enough, you must do what he says, attending to every word, taking every hint. If a hint is not taken, if a word is missed, it is lost forever; for he does not speak twice.

Jiddu Krishnamurti

At the Feet of the Master

Four qualifications there are for this pathway:

Discrimination

Desirelessness

Good conduct

Love

What the Master has said to me on each of these I shall try to tell you.

I

Discrimination

The first of these qualifications is discrimination; and this is usually taken as the discrimination between the real and the unreal which leads one to enter the Path. It is this, but it is also much more; and it is to be practiced, not only at the beginning of the Path, but at every step of it every day until the end. You enter the Path because you have learned that on it alone can be found those things which are worth gaining. Those who do not know, work to gain wealth and power, but these are at most for one life only, and therefore unreal. There are greater things than these—things which are real and lasting; when you have once seen these, you desire those others no more.

In all the world there are only two kinds of people—those who know, and those who do not know; and this knowledge is the thing which matters. What religion people hold, to what race they belong—these things are not important; the really important thing is this knowledge—the knowledge of God's plan for humanity. For God has a plan and that plan is evolution. When once we have seen that and really know it, we cannot help working for it and making ourselves one with it, because it is so glorious, so beautiful. So, because we know, we are on God's side, standing for good and resisting evil, working for evolution and not for selfishness.

Whoever is on God's side is one of us, and it does not matter in the least whether they call themselves Hindus, or Buddhists, Christians or Muslims, whether they are Indian or English, Chinese or Russian. Those who are on God's side know why they are here and what they should do, and they are trying to do it; all the others do not yet know what they should do, and so they often act foolishly, and try to invent ways for themselves which they think will be pleasant for themselves, not understanding that all are one, and that therefore only what the One wills can ever be really pleasant for anyone. They are following the unreal instead of the real. Until they learn to distinguish between these two, they have not ranged themselves on God's side, and so this discrimination is the first step.

But even when the choice is made, you must still remember that of the real and the unreal there are many varieties; and discrimination must still be made between the right and the wrong, the important and the unimportant, the useful and the useless, the true and the false, the selfish and the unselfish.

Between the right and wrong it should not be difficult to choose, for those who wish to follow the Master have already decided to take the right at all costs. But the body and the person are two, and the person's will is not always what the body wishes. When your body wishes something, stop and think whether *you* really wish it. For *you* are God, and you will only what God wills; but you must dig deep down into yourself to find the God within you, and listen to that voice, which is *your* voice. Do not mistake your bodies for yourself—neither the physical body, nor the astral, nor the mental. Each one of them will pretend to be the Self, in order to gain what it wants. But you must know them all, and know yourself as their master.

When there is work that must be done, the physical body wants to rest, to go out walking, to eat and drink; and the person who does not know says: "*I* want to do these things, and I must do them." But the person who knows says: "This that wants is *not* I, and it must wait awhile." Often when there is an opportunity to help someone, the body feels: "How much trouble it will be for me; let someone else do it." But the person replies to his body: "You shall not hinder me in doing good work."

The body is your animal—the horse upon which you ride. Therefore you must treat it well, and take good care of it; you must not overwork it, you must feed it properly on pure food and drink only, and keep it strictly clean always, even from the minutest speck of dirt. For without a perfectly clean and healthy body you cannot do the arduous work of preparation, you cannot bear its ceaseless strain. But it must always be you who control that body, not it that controls you.

The astral body has *its* desires—dozens of them; it wants you to be angry, to say sharp words, to feel jealous, to be greedy for money, to envy other people their possessions, to yield yourself to depression. All these things it wants, and many more, not because it wishes to harm you, but because it likes violent vibrations, and likes to change them constantly. But *you* want none of these things, and therefore you must discriminate between your wants and your body's.

Your mental body wishes to think itself proudly separate, to think much of itself and little of others. Even when you have turned it away from worldly things, it still tries to calculate for self, to make you think of your own progress, instead of thinking of the Master's work and of helping others. When you meditate, it will try to make you think of the many different things which *it* wants instead of the one thing which *you* want. You are not this mind, but it is yours to use; so here again discrimination is necessary. You must watch unceasingly, or you will fail.

Between right and wrong, the Path knows no compromise. At whatever apparent cost, that which is right you must do, that which is wrong you must not do, no matter what the ignorant may think or say. You must study deeply the hidden laws of nature, and when you know them arrange your life according to them, using always reason and common sense.

You must discriminate between the important and the unimportant. Firm as a rock where right and wrong are concerned, yield always to others in things which do not matter. For you must be always gentle and kindly, reasonable and accommodating, leaving to others the same full liberty which you need for yourself.

Try to see what is worth doing; and remember that you must not judge by the size of a thing. A small thing which is directly useful in the Master's work is far better worth doing than a large thing which the world would call good. You must distinguish not only the useful from the useless, but the more useful from the less useful. To feed the poor is a good and noble and useful work; yet to feed their souls is nobler and more useful than to feed their bodies. Any rich person can feed the body, but only those who know can feed the soul. If you know, it is your duty to help others to know.

However wise you may be already, on this Path you have much to learn; so much that here also there must be discrimination, and you must think carefully what is worth learning. All knowledge is useful, and one day you will have all knowledge; but while you have only part, take care that it is the most useful part. God is Wisdom as well as Love; and the more wisdom you have the more you can manifest of God. Study then, but study first that which will most help you to help others. Work patiently at your studies, not that others may think you wise, not even that you may have the happiness of being wise, but because only the wise person can be wisely helpful. However much you wish to help, if you are ignorant you may do more harm than good.

You must distinguish between truth and falsehood; you must learn to be true all through, in thought and word and deed.

In thought first; and that is not easy, for there are in the world many untrue thoughts, many foolish superstitions, and no one who is enslaved by them can make progress. Therefore you must not hold a thought just because many other people hold it, nor because it has been believed for centuries, nor because it is written in some book which people think sacred; you must think of the matter for yourself, and judge for yourself whether it is reasonable. Remember that though a thousand people agree upon a subject, if they know nothing about that subject their opinion is of no value. Those who would walk upon the Path must learn to think for themselves, for superstition is one of the greatest evils in the world, one of the fetters from which you must utterly free yourself.

Your thought about others must be true; you must not think of them what you do not know. Do not suppose that they are always thinking of you. If others do something which you think will harm you, or say something which you think applies to you, do not think at once: "They meant to injure me." Most probably they never thought of you at all, for each soul has its own troubles and its thoughts turn chiefly around itself. If others speak angrily to you, do not think: "They hate me, they wish to wound me." Probably some one or something else has made them angry, and because they happen to meet you they turn their anger upon you. They are acting foolishly, for all anger is foolish, but you must not therefore think untruly of them.

When you become a pupil of the Master, you may always try the truth of your thought by laying it beside his. For pupils are one with the Master, and they need only to put back their thought into the Master's thought to see at once whether it agrees. If it does not, it is wrong, and they change it instantly, for the Master's thought is perfect, because he knows all. Those who are not yet accepted by him cannot do quite this; but they may greatly help themselves by stopping often to think: "What would the Master think about this? What would the Master say or do under these circumstances?" For you must never do or say or think what you cannot imagine the Master as doing or saying or thinking.

You must be true in speech too—accurate and without exaggeration. Never attribute motives to others; only their Master knows their thoughts, and they may be acting from reasons which have never entered your mind. If you hear a story against any-one, do not repeat it; it may not be true, and even if it is, it is kinder to say nothing. Think well before speaking, lest you should fall into inaccuracy.

Be true in action; never pretend to be other than you are, for all pretence is a hindrance to the pure light of truth, which should shine through you as sunlight shines through clear glass.

You must discriminate between the self-ish and the unselfish. For selfishness has many forms, and when you think you have finally killed it in one of them, it arises in another as strongly as ever. But by degrees you will become so full of thought for the helping of others that there will be no room, no time, for any thought about yourself.

You must discriminate in yet another way. Learn to distinguish the God in everyone and everything, no matter how evil they or it may appear on the surface. You can help your brother or sister through that which you have in common with them, and that is the Divine Life; learn how to arouse that in them, learn how to appeal to that in them; so shall you save your brother and sister from wrong.

II

Desirelessness

There are many for whom the qualification of desirelessness is a difficult one, for they feel that they *are* their desires—that if their distinctive desires, their likings and dislikings, are taken away from them, there will be no self left. But these are only they who have not seen the Master; in the light of his holy presence all desire dies, but the desire to be like him. Yet before you have the happiness of meeting him face to face, you may attain desirelessness if you will.

Discrimination has already shown you that the things which most people desire, such as wealth and power, are not worth having; when this is really felt, not merely said, all desire for them ceases.

Thus far all is simple; it needs only that you should understand. But there are some who forsake the pursuit of earthly aims only in order to gain heaven, or to attain personal liberation from rebirth; into this error you must not fall. If you have forgotten self altogether, you cannot be thinking when that self should be set free, or what kind of heaven it shall have. Remember that *all* selfish desire binds, however high may be its object, and until you have got rid of it you are not wholly free to devote yourself to the work of the Master.

When all desires for self are gone, there may still be a desire to see the result of your work. If you help anybody, you want to *see* how much you have helped him; perhaps even you want him to see it too, and to be grateful. But this is still desire, and also want of trust. When you pour out your strength to help, there must be a result, whether you can see it or not; if you know the Law you know this must be so. So you must do right for the sake of the right, not in the hope of reward; you must work for the sake of the work, not in the hope of seeing the result; you must give yourself to the service of the world because you love it, and cannot help giving yourself to it.

Have no desire for psychic powers; they will come when the Master knows that it is best for you to have them. To force them too soon often brings in its train much trouble; often their possessor is misled by deceitful nature-spirits, or becomes conceited and thinks he cannot make a mistake; and in any case the time and strength that it takes to gain them might be spent in work for others. They will come in the course of development—they *must* come; and if the Master sees that it would be useful for you to have them sooner, he will tell you how to unfold them safely. Until then, you are better without them.

You must guard, too, against certain small desires which are common in daily life. Never wish to shine, or to appear clever; have no desire to speak. It is well to speak little; better still to say nothing, unless you are quite sure that what you wish to say is true, kind, and helpful. Before speaking, think carefully whether what you are going to say has those three qualities; if it has not, do not say it.

It is well to get used even now to thinking carefully before speaking; for when you reach initiation you must watch every word, lest you should tell what must not be told. Much common talk is unnecessary and foolish; when it is gossip, it is wicked. So be accustomed to listen rather than to talk; do not offer opinions unless directly asked for them. One statement of the qualifications gives them thus: to know, to dare, to will, and to be silent; and the last of the four is the hardest of them all.

Another common desire which you must sternly repress is the wish to meddle in other people's business. What other people do or say or believe is no affair of yours, and you must learn to let them absolutely alone. They have full right to free thought and speech and action, so long as they do not interfere with anyone else. You yourself claim the freedom to do what you think proper; you must allow the same freedom to them, and when they exercise it, you have no right to talk about them.

If you think they are doing wrong, and you can contrive an opportunity of privately and very politely telling them why you think so, it is possible that you may convince them; but there are many cases in which even that would be an improper interference. On no account must you go and gossip to some third person about the matter, for that is an extremely wicked action.

If you see a case of cruelty to a child or an animal, it is your duty to interfere. If you see anyone breaking the law of the country, you should inform the authorities. If you are placed in charge of other persons in order to teach them, it may become your duty gently to tell them of their faults. Except in such cases, mind your own business, and learn the virtue of silence.

III

Six Points of Conduct

The six points of conduct which are specially required are given by the Master as:

1. Self-control as to the mind
2. Self-control in action
3. Tolerance
4. Cheerfulness
5. One-pointedness
6. Confidence

[I know some of these are often translated differently, as are the names of the qualifications; but in all cases I am using the names which the Master himself employed when explaining them to me.]

1. *Self-control as to the mind*

The qualification of desirelessness shows that the astral body must be controlled; this shows the same thing as to the mental body. It means control of temper, so that you may feel no anger or impatience; of the mind itself, so that the thought may always be calm and unruffled; and (through the mind) of the nerves, so that they may be as little irritable as possible. This last is difficult, because when you try to prepare yourself for the Path, you cannot help making your body more sensitive, so that its nerves are easily disturbed by a sound or a shock and feel any pressure acutely; but you must do your best.

The calm mind means also courage, so that you may face without fear the trials and difficulties of the Path; it means also steadiness, so that you may make light of the troubles which come into everyone's life, and avoid the incessant worry over little things in which many people spend most of their time. The Master teaches that it does not matter in the least what happens to a person from the outside; sorrows, troubles, sicknesses, losses—all these must be as nothing to you, and must not be allowed to affect the calmness of your mind. They are the result of past actions, and when they come you must bear them cheerfully, remembering that all evil is transitory, and that your duty is to remain always joyous and serene. They belong to your previous lives, not to this; you cannot alter them, so it is useless to trouble about them. Think rather of what you are doing now, which will make the events of your next life, for that you can alter.

Never allow yourself to feel sad or depressed. Depression is wrong, because it infects others and makes their lives harder, which you have no right to do. Therefore if ever it comes to you, throw it off at once.

In yet another way you must control your thought; you must not let it wander. Whatever you are doing, fix your thought upon it, that it may be perfectly done; do not let your mind be idle, but keep good thoughts always in the background of it, ready to come forward the moment it is free.

Use your thought power every day for good purposes; be a force in the direction of evolution. Think each day of someone whom you know to be in sorrow, or suffering, or in need of help, and pour out loving thought upon him.

Hold back your mind from pride, for pride comes only from ignorance. Those who do not know think that they are great, that they have done this or that great thing; the wise person knows that only God is great, that all good work is done by God alone.

2. *Self-control in action*

If your thought is what it should be, you will have little trouble with your action. Yet remember that, to be useful to mankind, thought must result in action. There must be no laziness, but constant activity in good work. But it must be your *own* duty that you do—not another person's, unless with their permission and by way of helping them. Leave everyone to do their own work in their own way; be always ready to offer help where it is needed, but never interfere. For many people, the most difficult thing in the world to learn is to mind their own business; but that is exactly what you must do.

Because you try to take up higher work, you must not forget your ordinary duties, for until they are done you are not free for other service. You should undertake no new worldly duties; but those which you have already taken upon you, you must perfectly fulfill—all clear and reasonable duties which yourself recognize, that is, not imaginary duties which others try to impose upon you. If you are to be the Master's pupil, you must do ordinary work better than others, not worse; because you must do that also for his sake.

3. *Tolerance*

You must feel perfect tolerance for all, and a hearty interest in the beliefs of those of another religion, just as much as in your own. For their religion is a path to the highest, just as yours is. And to help all, you must understand all.

But in order to gain this perfect tolerance, you must yourself first be free from bigotry and superstition. You must learn that no ceremonies are necessary; else you will think yourself somehow better than those who do not perform them. Yet you must not condemn others who still cling to ceremonies. Let them do as they will; only they must not interfere with you who know the truth—they must not try to force upon you that which you have outgrown. Make allowance for everything; be kindly towards everything.

Now that your eyes are opened, some of your old beliefs, your old ceremonies, may seem to you absurd; perhaps, indeed, they really are so. Yet though you can no longer take part in them, respect them for the sake of those good souls to whom they are still important. They have their place, they have their use; they are like those double lines which guided you as a child to write straight and evenly, until you learned to write far better and more freely without them. There was a time when you needed them; but now that time is past.

A great Teacher once wrote: "When I was a child, I spake as a child, I understood as a child, I thought as a child; but when I became a man I put away childish things." Yet one who has forgotten childhood and lost sympathy with children is not one who can teach them or help them. So look kindly, gently, tolerantly upon all; but upon all alike, Buddhist or Hindu, Jain or Jew, Christian or Muslim.

4. Cheerfulness

You must bear your karma cheerfully, whatever it may be, taking it as an honor that suffering comes to you, because it shows that the Lords of Karma think you worth helping. However hard it is, be thankful that it is no worse. Remember that you are of but little use to the Master until your evil karma is worked out, and you are free. By offering yourself to him, you have asked that your karma may be hurried, and so now in one or two lives you work through what otherwise might have been spread over a hundred. But in order to make the best out of it, you must bear it cheerfully, gladly.

Yet another point. You must give up all feeling of possession. Karma may take from you the things which you like best—even the people whom you love most. Even then you must be cheerful—ready to part with anything and everything. Often the Master needs to pour out his strength upon others through his servant; he cannot do that if the servant yields to depression. So cheerfulness must be the rule.

5. *One-pointedness*

The one thing that you must set before you is to do the Master's work. Whatever else may come in your way to do, that at least you must never forget. Yet nothing else *can* come in your way, for all helpful, unselfish work is the Master's work, and you must do it for his sake. And you must give all your attention to each piece as you do it, so that it may be your very best. The same Teacher also wrote: "Whatsoever ye do, do it *heartily,* as to the Lord, and not unto men." Think how you would do a piece of work if you knew that the Master was coming at once to look at it; just in that way you must do all your work. Those who know most will most know all that that verse means. And there is another like it, much older: "Whatsoever thy hand findeth to do, do it with thy might."

One-pointedness means, too, that nothing shall ever turn you, even for a moment, from the Path upon which you have entered. No temptations, no worldly pleasures, no worldly affections even, must ever draw you aside. For you yourself must become one with the Path; it must be so much part of your nature that you follow it without needing to think of it, and cannot turn aside. You, the monad, have decided it; to break away from it would be to break away from yourself.

6. Confidence

You must trust your Master; you must trust yourself. If you have seen the Master, you will trust him to the uttermost, through many lives and deaths. If you have not yet seen him, you must still try to realize him and trust him, because if you do not, even he cannot help you. Unless there is perfect trust, there cannot be the perfect flow of love and power.

You must trust yourself. You say you know yourself too well? If you feel so, you do *not* know yourself; you know only the weak outer husk, which has fallen often into the mire. But *you*—the real you—you are a spark of God's own fire, and God, who is almighty, is in you, and because of that there is nothing that you cannot do if you will. Say to yourself: "What humans have done, a human can do. I am a human, yet also God in humanness; I can do this thing, and I will." For your will must be like tempered steel, if you would tread the Path.

IV

Love

Of all the qualifications, love is the most important, for if it is strong enough in us, it forces us to acquire all the rest, and all the rest without it would never be sufficient. Often it is translated as an intense desire for liberation from the round of births and deaths, and for union with God. But to put it in that way sounds selfish, and gives only part of the meaning. It is not so much desire as *will*, resolve, determination. To produce its result, this resolve must fill your whole nature, so as to leave no room for any other feeling. It is indeed the will to be one with God, not in order that you may escape from weariness and suffering, but in order that because of your deep love for God you may act with God and as God does. Because God is love, you, if you would become one with God, must be filled with perfect unselfishness and love also.

In daily life this means two things; first, that you shall be careful to do no hurt to any living thing; second, that you shall always be watching for an opportunity to help.

First, to do no hurt. Three sins there are which work more harm than all else in the world—gossip, cruelty, and superstition—because they are sins against love. Against these three those who would fill their hearts with the love of God must watch ceaselessly.

See what gossip does. It begins with evil thought, and that in itself is a crime. For in everyone and in everything there is good; in everyone and in everything there is evil. Either of these we can strengthen by thinking of it, and in this way we can help or hinder evolution; we can do the will of the Logos or we can resist it. If you think of the evil in another, you are doing at the same time three wicked things:

(1) You are filling your neighborhood with evil thought instead of with good thought, and so you are adding to the sorrow of the world.

(2) If there is in other persons the evil which you think, you are strengthening it and feeding it; and so you are making them worse instead of better. But generally the evil is not

there, and you have only fancied it; and then your wicked thought tempts them to do wrong, for if they are not yet perfect, you may make them that which you have thought them.

(3) You fill your own mind with evil thoughts instead of good; and so you hinder your own growth, and make yourself, for those who can see, an ugly and painful object instead of a beautiful and lovable one.

Not content with having done all this harm to themselves and to their victims, gossips try with all their might to make other people partners in their crime. Eagerly they tell their wicked tale to others, hoping that they will believe it; and then they join with them in pouring evil thought upon the poor sufferer. And this goes on day after day, and is done not by one person but by thousands. Do you begin to see how base, how terrible a sin this is? You must avoid it altogether. Never speak ill of anyone; refuse to listen when anyone else speaks ill of another, but gently say: "Perhaps this is not true, and even if it is, it is kinder not to speak of it."

Then as to cruelty. This is of two kinds, intentional and unintentional. Intentional cruelty is purposely to give pain to another living being; and that is the greatest of all sins—the work of a devil rather than a human being. You would say that no person could do such a thing; but people have done it often, and are daily doing it now. The inquisitors did it; many religious people did it in the name of their religion. Vivisectors do it; many schoolmasters do it habitually. All these people try to excuse their brutality by saying that it is the custom; but a crime does not cease to be a crime because many commit it. Karma takes no account of custom; and the karma of cruelty is the most terrible of all. In India at least there can be no excuse for such customs, for the duty of harmlessness is well-known to all. The fate of the cruel must fall also upon all who go out intentionally to kill God's creatures, and call it "sport."

Such things as these you would not do, I know; and for the sake of the love of God, when opportunity offers, you will speak clearly against them. But there is a cruelty in speech as well as in act; and a person who says a word with the intention to wound another is guilty of this crime. That, too, you would not do; but sometimes a careless word does as much harm as a malicious one.

So you must be on your guard against unintentional cruelty.

It comes usually from thoughtlessness. People are so filled with greed and avarice that they never even think of the suffering which they cause to others by paying too little, or by half-starving children. Others think only of their own lust, and care little how many souls and bodies they ruin in satisfying it. Just to save a few minutes' trouble, an employer does not pay workmen on the proper day, thinking nothing of the difficulties this brings upon them. So much suffering is caused just by carelessness—by forgetting to think how an action will affect others. But karma never forgets, and it takes no account of the fact that people forget. If you wish to enter the Path, you must think of the consequences of what you do, lest you should be guilty of thoughtless cruelty.

Superstition is another mighty evil, and has caused much terrible cruelty. The person who is a slave to it despises others who are wiser, tries to force them to do as he does. Think of the awful slaughter produced by the superstition that animals should be sacrificed, and by the still more cruel superstition that we need flesh for food. Think of the treatment which superstition has meted out to the depressed classes in our beloved India, and see in that how this evil quality can breed heartless cruelty even among those who know the duty of brotherhood. Many crimes have been committed in the name of the God of love, moved by this nightmare of superstition; be very careful therefore that no slightest trace of it remains in you.

These three great crimes you must avoid, for they are fatal to all progress, because they sin against love. But not only must you thus refrain from evil; you must be active in doing good. You must be so filled with the intense desire of service that you are ever on the watch to render it to all around you—not to people alone, but even to animals and plants. You must render it in small things every day, that the habit may be formed, so that you may not miss the rare opportunity when the great thing offers itself to be done. For if you yearn to be one with God, it is not for your own sake; it is that you may be a channel through which his love may flow to reach your fellows.

Those who are on the Path exist not for themselves, but for others; they have forgotten themselves, in order that they may serve others. They are as a pen in the hand of God, through which the divine thought may flow, and find for itself an expression down here, which without a pen it could not have. Yet at the same time they are also a living plume of fire, raying out upon the world the Divine Love which fills their hearts.

The wisdom which enables you to help, the will which directs the wisdom, the love which inspires the will—these are your qualifications. Will, wisdom and love are the three aspects of the Logos; and you, who wish to enroll yourselves to serve the Logos, must show forth these aspects in the world.

Waiting the word of the Master,
Watching the hidden Light;
Listening to catch his orders
In the very midst of the fight;

Seeing his slightest signal
Across the heads of the throng;
Hearing his faintest whisper
Above earth's loudest song.

towards discipleship

The Origin of This Talk

In 1924, Krishnamurti spent six weeks (August 18 to September 28) in an eleventh-century castle remodeled as a hotel, in Pergine, a town in the northern part of Italy. He was accompanied by twelve others: his brother Nitya-nanda, John Cordes, Lady Emily Lutyens, V. C. Padwardhan and his wife Malati, D. Rajagopal, N. S. Rama Rao, Dr. N. Sivakamu (the eldest sister of Rukmini Arundale), and four girls: Helen Knothe, Elisabeth and Mary Lutyens (daughters of Lady Emily), and Ruth Roberts.

The time in Pergine was part vacation and part spiritual preparation. One of the participants described their stay as follows: "Our life here is one of intense inner activity and almost complete outer inertia" (Jayakar 58). A typical day went thus:

8:00 Meditation, with Krishnamurti reading a passage from *The Gospel According to Buddha,* followed by his, Nityananda's, and Rama Rao's chanting a mantra.

8:30 Breakfast, followed by a walk and games such as volleyball or rounders (a British version of baseball). During the latter part of their stay, Krishnamurti added an hour's talk on the Masters and the Path of Discipleship.

12:30 Lunch, followed by rest or
     individual work.
3:00 More games, followed by bathing.
6:00 Dinner, followed by "intensive
     preparation."
8:30 Bed.

Part of Krishnamurti's tutelage was especially directed to the four girls, who were preparing to go to Sydney, Australia, for further training by C. W. Leadbeater. In private talks, Krishnamurti alternately inspired them to dedication and criticized them for their faults (Lutyens, *Open Door* 9–12). He frequently despaired of the ability of his tutees to change: "You are like people in a dark room waiting for someone to turn on the light for you instead of groping in the dark and turning it on for yourselves" (Lutyens, *Years of Awakening* 193).

During the stay at Pergine, Krishnamurti's "process" restarted and lasted from August 21 to September 24. This "process" was an experience of great pain for Krishnamurti, but also culminated in contact with the Masters. (Aryal Sanat discusses the "process" comprehensively in *The Inner Life of Krishnamurti*.) After the final night of this session of the "process," Krishnamurti reported a visit from the Master Maitreya, who left this message (Lutyens, *Years of Awakening* 193–4):

Learn to serve Me, for along that path alone will you find me
Forget yourself, for then only am I to be found

Do not look for the Great Ones when
   they may be very near you
You are like the blind man who seeks
   sunshine
You are like the hungry man who is
   offered food and will not eat
The happiness you seek is not far off;
   it lies in every common stone
I am there if you will only see. I am
   the Helper if you will let Me help.

The morning talks were written down in longhand by one of the participants and later published as a book, *Towards Discipleship*, in the preface to which (vii–viii) Krishnamurti described the time at Pergine and the resulting book as follows:

At Pergine was one of the happiest summers that my brother and I had spent, and when we had left that ideally beautiful spot, he and I used to talk about our stay there, the distant lake and the snow-clad mountains. A new life began for us at Pergine castle, and I hope all those that were there with us will feel the same.

These personal talks were given to friends, and not to a general audience. Later on some of these friends suggested that our talks should be brought out in the form of a little book. Had I known that our morning talks were going to appear as a book, I certainly would have been more careful in the expressions of my thought.

So I beg my readers to remember that all the talks were extremely informal and unconventional. But I hope they will be useful.

The first talk begins with Krishnamurti's response to the question "What are the special qualifications which should be acquired before Probation, Acceptance and Initiation?" His answer begins, "The essential qualifications to aim at before Probation are: (1) Unselfishness, (2) Plenty of affection of the right sort, and (3) Capacity for sympathy." He continues through fifteen talks in commenting on such qualifications, which complement the four qualifications of *At the Feet of the Master.* Krishnamurti gave these talks at the age of 29, about 14 years after receiving the instructions of *At the Feet of the Master*, published in 1910.

A comparison of the two sets of qualifications shows certain consistencies, but also some differences. The earlier qualifications are traditional ones restated for and by a boy. The later set are more in Krishnamurti's own voice. The final, sixteenth talk of the series, summarizing the whole, is presented here for contrast with the four qualifications of *At the Feet of the Master* and as an example of Krishnamurti's development between his own stage of pupilage and his later position of independence.

Eight Further Qualifications
for the Path

KRISHNAJI: This is our last collective talk, and so it will be just as well if we went over all the reasons why we are here, and how we hope to attain what we desire.

I think it is quite obvious that all of us here will some day be taken on as probationary pupils by various Masters. And it is also quite obvious that we all want to get on so as to get nearer the Masters, for that is what matters and nothing else. But to get near the Masters we must have the right desire, combined with efforts which must be one-pointed and constant, and not depending on our moods or feelings.

It is clear that what we have to do is to forget ourselves, our personal wants and desires, and get to the main purpose, which is to reach the Masters and to serve them. To be able to forget ourselves, we must have very thoroughly and clearly some of the rudimentary qualities which we all know we lack, and also get rid of certain others which we have. We must have certain weaknesses completely destroyed, so that they may not unexpectedly crop up when we are relaxing, or we do not quite feel well or when we are tired.

The first thing, it seems to me, is to destroy absolutely the self, and not to allow any trace of any kind of selfishness, by examining every door through which selfishness can enter. Put a sentinel at each door to keep out selfishness. There is a strong element of selfishness in all of us. We can see in our daily actions how it is a strong and prevailing element. It is clear, all the same, that it is not the qualities so much as the attitude which takes one nearer the Masters. But to get the attitude, we must have a certain foundation of qualities.

We must have drilled into each one of us a distinct idea that we cannot at any period or any given moment be possibly selfish, either in little things or in big things; because that is going to keep us back. The self is hidden away in each one of us. It wants digging up to discover it. We must mercilessly root it out, destroy it, so that selfishness shall not be part of our further evolutionary course. There are one or two in whom selfishness is not so predominant, but in the majority of us it is. If we do not take care, while we are young and full of enthusiasm, it will be like a weight tied to our feet later when we want to fly. At a later stage it will be much harder.

It is one of the most rudimentary requirements that a pupil should be unselfish. The reason is the Master cannot be a guide to us, cannot influence us, if we cannot love, cannot be affectionate; and we cannot be that if we are selfish and self-centered. It is not obvious to every one that selfishness in little things is a sin against God, a sin against the Master. C.W.L. used all the time to din into Nitya and me from morning till night that we were pupils of the Master, and that there must be no thought of selfishness in us.

Each one of us must go about the matter intelligently, determined to find out the self from each corner or lurking place, and destroy it. A selfish man can never advance, never make progress, because spirituality does not come near him or lend itself to him. It is the man who is open, clear, frank, unselfish that advances. Most of us live in a kind of hot, uncomfortable atmosphere; some of us carry that influence of discomfort about with us, because we have not caught the vision or have any idea of the immense possibilities of unselfishness. Each one of us must be like the fresh North Wind. And we cannot mark time.

Each one of us must be very careful of this matter of selfishness and unselfishness. You have no idea how unexpectedly selfishness can crop up. When you have no idea you are selfish, you will find the self to be dominant. The more you advance the greater is the possibility of your fall, and the possibility of a fall for every person advancing on the Path of spirituality lies chiefly through selfishness. We, who are just beginning, who have just caught the glimpse from the top of the mountain, must be careful, extra careful, to get rid of selfishness. If you have got rid of selfishness, the gates of heaven will never be kept closed against you.

To attain to a perfection in unselfishness, we must work upon other qualities in us. The other qualities are as follows.

1. *Affection.*

That first means liking everybody and being friends with all; but it is more than that, for it is also having the capacity to give a deep affection to another. It does not mean walking arm in arm, or clinging affectionately, and so on. It means you must desire to give the best of yourself to another.

We sometimes feel we cannot get on with certain persons. But we must be affectionate to all. Also, we do not have sufficient capacity to return the love that is given to us. Not that anybody gives us love with the hope of its return, but for our part, we must have the capacity to return love the moment it is given. We must react to it quickly. We must be bubbling over with it, instead of which we just remain callous, or else think about ourselves, our sentimental nature, etc., when, in reality, we ought to be giving in return something of our own. Everybody is capable of love of a certain kind, even if it be the lowest form of a sexual kind. But even so it is there. We can make our love glow like a lighthouse, or let it get dim like a candle.

For each one of us, if we are going to follow the Path, unless we are very careful, it is going to be a very lonely life. Everybody is interested in the work, and nobody in the personality. So if we do not fit into a work, naturally the person who is better suited to it will take our place, and we shall find ourselves kind of left out. That is where we must be very careful. After we have given up the outer world and come up halfway to the world of spirituality, we shall then be terribly lonely, and come to that moment when we begin to suppress our feelings, because it is the easiest way of getting rid of feelings. So what was a rose and a beautiful thing is destroyed, and we have to build it up again. Each one of us must guard against that and be careful that we make it every day a practice of loving some-one, of giving something of our affection to somebody.

2. *Purity.*

Then we must be absolutely pure. The more we advance, the greater must be our purity. Most of us want affection in return. The more affectionate you are the greater must be the restraint on the self, because affection mixed with selfishness becomes gross and unclean. Our affections must be pure, if we are to become, as we must, the embodiment of Love. This is all so simple and clear, and so common; yet we begin to lose sight of it all and become complicated, and think of things that do not matter.

3. *Sympathy.*

Then, if you have affection, real affection, you are bound to have sympathy which enables you to give something you have or something you have felt to another. We have all been told these things here over and over again. Perhaps nobody asks you for anything, but you must be ready always to give what you have by your look, by your gesture, by your willingness of behavior. You must have more and more of these things as your background so that they may be evoked at the slightest call. We have these qualities, but we are so engrossed in our own selfishness and ambition that they all get submerged and vanish.

Affection, reverence and devotion, all follow in each other's footsteps. The person who lacks affection, begins to lack reverence, because his mind becomes conceited and he cannot find anybody bigger than himself to admire. If you realize these things, and have these essentials at your fingers' ends, you will want your body to be under your perfect guidance and control. A flower washed by the rain and wind, have you ever seen it dirty? Our garden needs to be purified and cultivated. Instead of keeping pure in our perennial beauty, we surround ourselves with all sorts of dirt.

4. *Tidiness*.

Again, you want to be tidy. Because it shows your attitude. You must dress well, look well and clean. You must have the desire to be clean and neat and tidy as the Master is. It is the sloppy mind and the sloppy brain, which denote a lack of the right desire. But your idea and your desire must not be only in clothes, like the women whose temple is Bond Street. I want to be the best dressed man, because the Master is well dressed. The way you comb your hair, the way you put on your shoes and walk, every detail, however small, is of importance. C.W.L. used to "go" for us when we tied our laces badly or our hair was untidy. Mind you, it does not matter eventually, but it does at the beginning far more than one thinks. And you must keep your body well and healthy for the sake of the Master. Your whole being exists for the Master. You must have a body that responds, that has fiber and stamina, and is not like soft pudding. Everything matters—how you look, how you smile and talk and behave, what your manners are, everything. We are all wanting to get up on the mountain top, and yet we do not know how to tie our shoelaces. How do you expect the Master to come near any of us if our minds, our emotions, our whole being, are all in a whirl?

5. *Adaptability.*

But although we must have everything pigeonholed, we must avoid getting into ruts. You must not go to extremes. You must be tidy, but do not let everybody notice that you are all the time trying to be that. Your mind should not fall into a groove, an invariable mold. But when the Master requires it, it should become untidy, so that new ideas, new inspirations, can come in. It must be elastic. And it is the same with emotions.

6. *Balance*.

There is not fiber enough in our makeup. There is not that stamina that makes great men. We are easily depressed one moment, and elated another. One day something affects us one way and another day the same thing affects us in a different way. How easily one becomes depressed; yet there is no greater enemy that keeps one away from the Master than depression. It is like a cloud passing over the sun and darkening everything. It is the one thing you should be above. Yet each day we feel miserable, or lonely, and so hardly make any progress. If we have the right attitude we cannot help being cheerful and happy.

7. *Distinction*.

We must not be *bourgeois*, a mixture of good, bad, and indifferent, a mixture of negatives and positives. A Master does not want a pupil of that kind. He can find better examples of humanity than that. What he wants is a person who says: "I am willing to be made into anything you want of me." If you have that, you have as good as got all the qualities required. If you are a real devotee, every breath of wind, a cloud, the blue sky, will have something to give you, and will, in some measure, make of you what he wants.

You do not know what we are missing every day by letting the little things overpower us. It happened the other day that the Master was with us for some time, and yet very few of us recognized him or realized the fact. We have not the capacity to recognize such a being when he is near us, because of the old habit, which we know so well, of going round and round ourselves, which makes us so miserable and makes others also so miserable. Some of us have not yet the rudiments, the very essentials, of discipleship.

We have each one of us something definite to learn and something definite to give, and that is ourselves—our love, our devotion, everything that is great about us. And we must learn everything that the Master wants, and not go on picking up rubbish here and there. We must have all these things somewhere carefully treasured at the back of us, so that we can always rely on ourselves and be a lamp unto ourselves. It is like living in a beautiful garden, so that when you are tired you can go and rest in it.

8. *Self-recollectedness.*

We have not learned to separate the body from the soul, the ugly from the beautiful, and yet we want to approach the Master. Every day that passes without true self-recollected-ness is a day wasted, is a day spent, not for the Master, but for yourself, a day spent, not in his service, but in seeking your own vain and self-ish end.

You must have in your garden all the wonderful things which each one of us can possibly develop. They are already there, but they are locked up for lack of expression. Make your garden more and more beautiful, and one day it will be so wonderful that the world will come and look at it, whereas now no one cares a rap whether you have a garden or not, or what flowers it contains. We must separate the soul, the wonderful garden with all the beautiful things which it contains—its pure emotions, beautiful thoughts, and great affections—from the selfishness of the self. If you are a mixture of both, it will take years even to acknowledge to yourself the distinction between the two, and to act on that distinction. These two things are as clear as night and day, and yet we are wasting time and energy by not acting.

Every effort in the right direction clears our vision of the Truth. Instead of going about, metaphorically, with locked jaws and clenched teeth and tense muscles, if we went about naturally and simply, keeping the goal constantly in front of our eyes, we should get there in no time. We are careless, slack, and we suddenly drop everything. The next day, even if we are not slack, the lost moment will not come back again. We should be above these fluctuations. When the World Teacher is here, the day we are tired and slack we shall be useless. It will be a wonderful day outside, and we shall be locked up in a room. That is what we are all doing—one day, we are under a clear sky and breathing pure air, and the next day we are locking ourselves in a room without a current of air.

We are all intelligent, but now we have come to the stage when we must emerge out of the limitations of the self, if our intelligence is to be of any use to us. What we want is the desire and the power and the determination to remain always in the garden, and to direct our love and devotion and service from the garden and not from the house. And now is coming the time to test what each one of us is truly worth. Now comes the time when we should use all our power of mind and emotions in cultivating our garden, and not let a day, a single second, pass without working in the garden and making an improvement here and there. The more you make the garden wonderful, the more weeds you take out, the greater will be the attraction and the beauty of it. And on each one of us depends the glorification and the beautifying of that garden. We must not really lose a single second. You do not know what beauty there is ahead of us; and every second that we pass without self-recollectedness amounts in a measure to a denial of that beauty.

After all, we are all here eventually to serve the Teacher when he comes. We should be like wonderful flowers, radiating delicious perfumes wherever we go; and we should be able to do so if we have cultivated and beautified our garden. Then it does not matter where we are, London or Adyar or Sydney or Pergine or the slums. See to it that you make that garden so beautiful that it becomes a fit sanctuary for the Master, a place wherein your friends—and even your foes—may come in perpetual adoration and in the attitude of worship.

IV

References and Further Reading

Jayakar, Pupul. *Krishnamurti: A Biography*. San Francisco: Harper & Row, 1986.

Lutyens, Mary. *Krishnamurti: The Open Door*. New York: Farrar Straus Giroux, 1988.

———. *Krishnamurti: The Years of Awakening*. New York: Farrar Straus Giroux, 1975.

Krishnamurti, Jiddu. *At the Feet of the Master*. Adyar: The Theosophist Office, 1910.

———. *Commentaries on Living: From the Notebooks of J. Krishnamurti*. 3 Series. Ed. D. Rajagopal. Wheaton, IL: Theosophical Publishing House, Quest Books, 1967.

——. *Towards Discipleship: A Series of Informal Addresses to Aspirants for Discipleship*. Adyar: Theosophical Publishing House, 1925.

——, Mabel Collins, and H. P. Blavatsky. *Inspirations from Ancient Wisdom: At the Feet of the Master; Light on the Path; The Voice of the Silence*. Wheaton, IL: Theosophical Publishing House, Quest Books, 1999.

Ravindra, Ravi. *Krishnamurti: Two Birds on One Tree*. Wheaton, IL: Theosophical Publishing House, Quest Books, 1995.

Sanat, Aryel. *The Inner Life of Krishnamurti: Private Passion and Perennial Wisdom*. Wheaton, IL: Theosophical Publishing House, Quest Books, 1999.